Seven Wonders of
ANCIENT CENTRAL
and SOUTH AMERICA

Michael Woods and Mary B. Woods

TWENTY-FIRST CENTURY BOOKS

Minneapolis

To Jacqueline Rosen and Lynette Curran

Twenty-First Century Books
A division of Lerner Publishing Group, Inc.
241 First Avenue North
Minneapolis, MN 55401 U.S.A.

Website address: www.lernerbooks.com

Library of Congress Cataloging-in-Publication Data

Woods, Michael, 1946–
    Seven wonders of ancient Central and South America / by Michael Woods and Mary B. Woods.
       p.   cm. – (Seven wonders)
    Includes bibliographical references and index.
    ISBN 978–0–8225–7570–2 (lib. bdg. : alk. paper)
    1. Indians of Central America—Antiquities—Juvenile literature. 2. Indians of South America—Antiquities—Juvenile literature. I. Woods, Mary B. (Mary Boyle), 1946– II. Title.
    F1434.W66 2009
    980–dc22   2007047824

Manufactured in the United States of America
1 2 3 4 5 6 – DP – 14 13 12 11 10 09

Contents

INTRODUCTION

*P*EOPLE LOVE TO MAKE LISTS OF THE BIGGEST AND THE BEST. ALMOST 2,500 YEARS AGO, A GREEK WRITER NAMED HERODOTUS MADE A LIST OF THE MOST AWESOME THINGS EVER BUILT BY PEOPLE. THE LIST INCLUDED BUILDINGS, STATUES, AND OTHER OBJECTS THAT WERE LARGE, WONDROUS, AND IMPRESSIVE. OTHER WRITERS ADDED THEIR OWN IDEAS TO THE LIST. THE WRITERS EVENTUALLY AGREED ON A FINAL LIST. IT WAS CALLED THE SEVEN WONDERS OF THE ANCIENT WORLD. THE ANCIENT WONDERS WERE:

THE GREAT PYRAMID AT GIZA: *a tomb for an ancient Egyptian king. The pyramid still stands in Giza, Egypt.*

THE COLOSSUS OF RHODES: *a giant bronze statue of Helios, the Greek sun god. The statue stood in Rhodes, an island in the Aegean Sea.*

THE LIGHTHOUSE AT ALEXANDRIA: *an enormous beacon to sailors at sea. It stood in the harbor in Alexandria, Egypt.*

THE HANGING GARDENS OF BABYLON: *magnificent gardens in the ancient city of Babylon (near modern-day Baghdad, Iraq)*

THE MAUSOLEUM AT HALICARNASSUS: *a marble tomb for a ruler in the Persian Empire. It was located in the ancient city of Halicarnassus (in modern Turkey).*

THE STATUE OF ZEUS AT OLYMPIA: *a statue honoring the king of the Greek gods. It stood in Olympia, Greece.*

THE TEMPLE OF ARTEMIS AT EPHESUS: *a temple honoring a Greek goddess. It stood on the coast of the Aegean Sea, in modern-day Turkey.*

Most of these ancient wonders are no longer standing. Wars, earthquakes, weather, and the passage of time destroyed them. Over the years, people made other lists of wonders. They listed wonders of the modern world and wonders of the natural world. They even listed wonders for each continent on Earth. This book is about the wonders of ancient Central and South America.

A WONDERFUL PLACE

Central America is part of the North American continent. It stretches from Guatemala and Belize, bordering Mexico, to the southern border of Panama. The continent of South America includes the whole landmass south of Panama. These two regions are often grouped together because they were both colonized largely by the Spanish.

European explorers first landed on the shores of Central and South America around 1500. As they traveled around the New World (as they called it), they discovered bustling civilizations of native people. Civilizations are organized societies. They have governments, cities, roads, writing systems, art and culture, science, a steady food supply, and armies to protect themselves.

Some of the world's oldest and most advanced civilizations lived in Central and South America. The Maya made books from tree bark and filled them with hieroglyphic (picture) writing about their history and ideas. These civilizations also made impressive contributions to the fields of agriculture, art, sports, science, architecture, and more.

A TRIP BACK IN TIME

Get ready to visit some of the wonders of ancient Central and South America. *Ancient* is another word for "old"—so we will explore cities, temples, monuments, and other wonders from long ago. One stop will be a royal city, lost for centuries among the mountains of Peru. We will also visit an area of land used as the world's largest ancient sketch pad. Other stops will include a giant stone staircase and a town of monstrous statues. Get ready for adventure—and some surprises—as you begin your tour of ancient Central and South America.

A carved stela from Tiwanaku, Bolivia

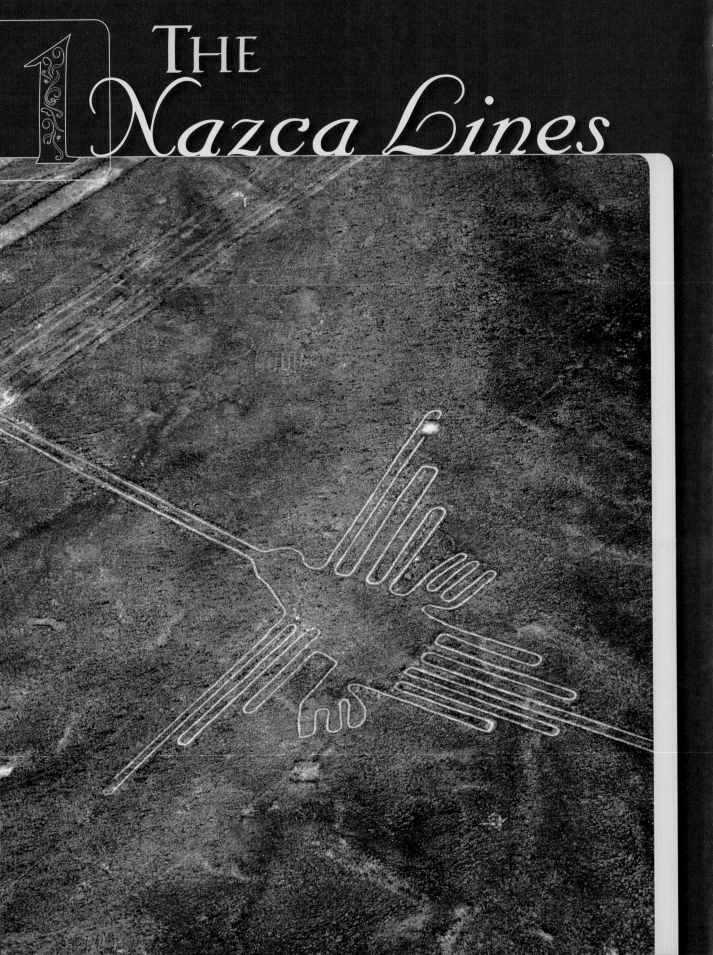

1 THE Nazca Lines

$\mathcal{A}$RCHAEOLOGIST TRIBIO MEJÍA XESSPE STOOD ON A HILLTOP IN SOUTHERN PERU IN THE 1920s. PLAINS AND HILLS OF THE NAZCA DESERT SPRAWLED AROUND HIM AS FAR AS THE EYE COULD SEE. FROM THE GROUND BELOW, WHERE MEJÍA XESSPE WAS WORKING ON AN ARCHAEOLOGY DIG, THE LAND SEEMED MOSTLY BARE. BUT LOOKING DOWN FROM THE HILL, MEJÍA XESSPE SPOTTED SOMETHING ASTOUNDING.

Huge lines, shapes, and drawings sprawled across the ground, as if a giant with a sharp stick had used the land as a sketch pad. These have become known as the Nazca Lines. This art gallery in the desert features a pelican five times larger than a modern Boeing 747 jumbo jet. The bird's wings—935 feet (285 meters) across—would cover three high school football fields.

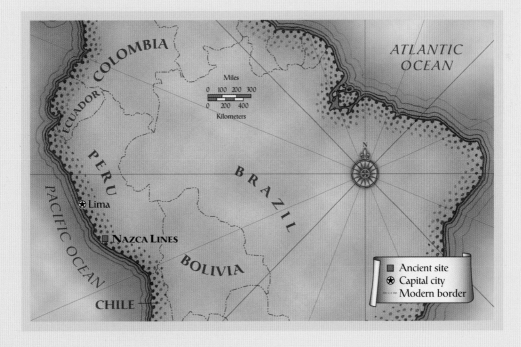

The Nazca people of Peru created a number of large designs, such as this giant spiral-tailed monkey, on the desert floor. About eighty thousand tourists per year view the lines from the air.

One colossal monkey is the size of a football field. About one thousand lines and objects are etched in the desert over an area of 400 square miles (1,036 square kilometers). They include a gigantic spider, a lizard, a dog, a killer whale, a figure that looks like an astronaut, flowers, straight lines, spirals, rectangles, and zigzags.

Mejía Xesspe might have been among the first people to see the Nazca lines from above. Pilots flying over the area in the 1920s and 1930s noticed the lines, and they helped scientists discover more. People of the Nazca civilization dug these mysterious lines between 200 B.C. and A.D. 600.

GREAT *Geoglyphs*

The Nazca lines are the world's most famous geoglyphs. *Geo* means "ground" and *glyph* means "drawing." However, these ground drawings certainly are not the world's only geoglyphs. Other strange drawings appear elsewhere in South America and in the United States, Japan, and Europe.

The Nazca left no written records, and we know very little about their civilization. Since the Nazca people thrived in one of the world's driest deserts, they must have been excellent farmers and builders. Archaeologists have found ruins of irrigation systems, built to water crops.

Pictures on ancient Nazca pottery show that they probably worshipped many gods. Some of the gods looked fierce and frightening. Pictures of these gods had huge eyes, fanglike teeth, and bodies that were half cat and half human.

From ancient mummies found in graves in the area, archaeologists can also tell that the Nazca people respected their dead. People were buried with love and care. Relatives wrapped the bodies in blankets woven with beautiful designs.

A Nazca artist depicted a fanciful and frightening bird-god with a human face on this two-spouted ceramic jug (right). *The Nazca also made wonderful textiles. This mummy* (below) *was carefully wrapped in a handmade blanket.*

ARTISTS FROM OUTER SPACE?

When standing on the ground, the Nazca people could not see an entire drawing of a monkey or dog. This area has hills but no high mountains from which to look down. And in those days, of course, there were no airplanes.

So how did they create such shapes without being able to see the entire drawing? Did the Nazca really make the drawings?

At first, no one had a clear answer to those questions. The Swiss explorer and writer Erich von Daniken suggested in 1968 that aliens visiting Earth from other planets had made the lines. Von Daniken thought that aliens in flying saucers beamed down instructions for the drawings. He thought that aliens used some of the straight lines as landing strips for their spacecraft.

The mysterious size and nature of the ancient lines have caused many people to wonder who created them and why. Erich von Daniken (below) promoted the idea that aliens made the lines to be used as landing strips.

Scientists, however, say that idea is silly. They are sure that the Nazca people made the lines. The Nazca certainly had a perfect scratch pad, thanks to the soil and weather conditions that existed in the Peruvian desert.

Ground in the area is covered with dark-colored stones. Soil underneath the stones is a lighter color. By sweeping away rows of the stones, the Nazca people could easily make visible lines. They piled the cleared stones along the edge of each line to make a clear outline.

In other parts of the world, the Nazca lines soon would have disappeared. Rain and wind would have filled them in with dirt. The lines remained visible here because of the Nazca desert's climate. With so little rain, erosion from water never erased the lines. The area also had very little wind to blow dirt or sand that might cover up the lines.

Could the ancient Nazca people have seen their lines from the air? An explorer and writer named Jim Woodman showed that it might have been possible. In 1975 Woodman flew a hot-air balloon that he constructed from cotton cloth and other materials that would have been available to the Nazca people. Nobody knows, however, if the Nazca people ever built such a balloon.

TEMPLES THAT WALKED?

People often make drawings and other works of art to look at and enjoy. Why would an ancient civilization bother to make drawings that could be appreciated only from the air? Since the Nazca people left no written records, we may never know for sure. However, many archaeologists think that the lines had to do with Nazca religious beliefs.

Some ancient civilizations believed that the sun and the moon were eyes of gods that lived in the sky and looked down on Earth. The Nazca people might have built the figures to please their gods or as prayers or messages to those gods. Some religious people in Peru still believe that drawings of spiders and monkeys have special religious and magical powers.

The Nazca could have used the figures in a form of prayer. Some experts suggest that people with lighted torches might have paraded back and forth along the lines while chanting or praying. What would the Nazca people have wanted from their gods?

Perhaps they were praying for water. Life in this desert depended on water. The arms and heads on some animals seem to point toward underground wells.

"I'm sure Egypt's pyramid builders could never have worked blindfolded—never having been able to stand back and admire their work. I felt the people who built Nazca had to have seen it. It is all just too incredible to have never been seen or admired by its creators."

—*Jim Woodman,* Nazca: Journey to the Sun, *1977*

A Nazca spider geoglyph crawls across the Peruvian desert.

Suppose those wells went dry during a long drought. The Nazca people might have drawn figures they believed were magical, such as monkeys and spiders. Those animals might have signaled to the gods that certain wells needed to be refilled.

ANCIENT CALENDAR?

Maria Reiche, a German mathematician, thought the lines had a different purpose. Reiche began to study the Nazca lines in 1946. Unable to see the lines clearly from the ground, Reiche asked the Peruvian air force for help. Air force pilots took photos of the lines. Those photos helped Reiche to make maps of the area. She got an idea.

<blockquote>
"It seems almost incredible that ground drawings made by superficially scratching the surface could have withstood the ravages of time and weather over such long periods."

—*Maria Reiche, 1949*
</blockquote>

Reiche realized that the Nazca might have used the lines as a calendar. They could have tracked the sun's movements across the lines. That would have helped them monitor the seasons of the year. They would know when to plant crops and when to celebrate festivals and other important events.

Reiche described these ideas in a book, *Mystery on the Desert*. The book became very popular. Reiche used profits from the book to help preserve the lines. She hired guards to keep people from damaging the lines. Reiche also encouraged the government of Peru to protect this wonder.

Maria Reiche (above, photographed in 1988) *moved to Peru in 1932. She spent most of her life studying and helping to preserve the Nazca lines.*

NO ALIENS NEEDED

Archaeologists know that the Nazca people could have drawn the lines without help from flying saucers. Creating long, straight lines requires just two wooden stakes and string. One person pounds a stake into the ground, ties the string onto it, and stretches the string into the distance. A second person makes sure the string is straight. Then the end of the string is tied around a second stake. The remains of stakes have been found near some of the Nazca lines.

Monkeys, spiders, and other complicated designs could have been made from a grid (a set of crisscrossing lines that form squares) of wooden stakes and strings. Modern quilt makers enlarge their patterns in this same way. They draw the pattern onto a grid. Then they redraw the design on a grid with larger squares.

In 1984 a scientific expedition in Peru showed that figures could have been drawn even without a pattern. In only ninety minutes, they made a straight line 40 feet (12 m) long and 3.3 feet (1 m) wide—ending in a spiral 115 feet (35 m) long.

A Modern Wonder

Although there are no surviving Nazca people in modern times, scientists can still learn about their culture by studying the Nazca lines. The mysterious designs have also brought other curious visitors to Peru. Thousands of tourists visit the area each year.

However, modern civilization is threatening this ancient wonder. Mining companies have opened mines near some of the Nazca figures. Trucks traveling to and from the mines have left tire marks on the land. And sometimes tourists or locals drive across the lines as shortcuts. Unusually wet weather in the late 1990s also caused damage. Floods and mud slides washed away parts of several Nazca figures.

Scientists must find ways to preserve the area. They have already built an observation deck, where people can view several designs without adding their footprints to the ancient artwork. But people must keep working to protect the Nazca lines. The mysteries of this ancient wonder are sure to keep unfolding.

An illegal road made by local residents cuts across a geoglyph of a dog. In 1994 the United Nations Educational, Scientific, and Cultural Organization (UNESCO) named the 175-square-mile (282 sq. km) protected zone a World Heritage Site. But the Nazca lines are in danger of disappearing because of careless tourists and local traffic. The Pan-American Highway, a network of roads running from Alaska to southern South America, cuts through one of the geoglyphs.

2 MACHU *Picchu*

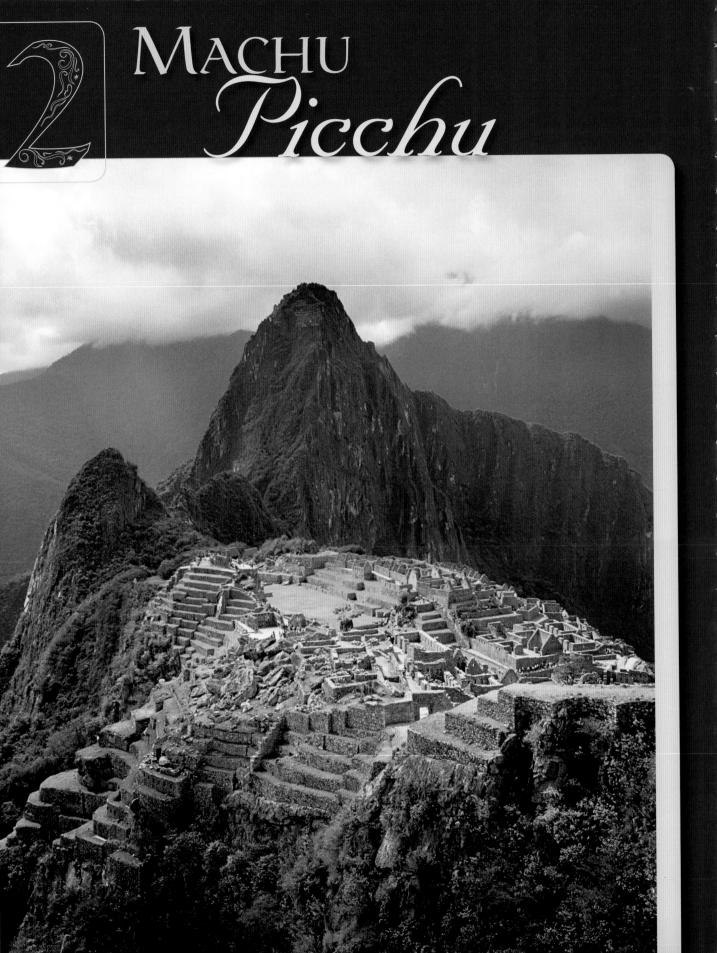

*I*N A.D. 1438, THE WARRIOR YUPANQUI BECAME KING OF THE INCA PEOPLE IN MODERN-DAY PERU. HE MUST HAVE PREDICTED BIG THINGS FOR HIMSELF. THE NEW KING TOOK A ROYAL NAME, PACHACUTI, WHICH MEANS "EARTH SHAKER." PACHACUTI CERTAINLY SHOOK UP THE INCA.

This great warrior king conquered other people who lived along the Andes Mountains in Peru. In doing so, he started building the ancient Inca Empire. It became the biggest and richest empire of its time. The city of Cuzco became its capital.

Pachacuti wanted a place for the royal family to stay when it was away from Cuzco. Perhaps he wanted a center for religious worship or just a getaway spot. Pachacuti chose a place about 50 miles (80 km) from Cuzco. But building one huge palace there would have been difficult. It was a narrow ridge of land between two soaring mountain peaks, Machu Picchu (Old Mountain) and Huayna Picchu (New Mountain).

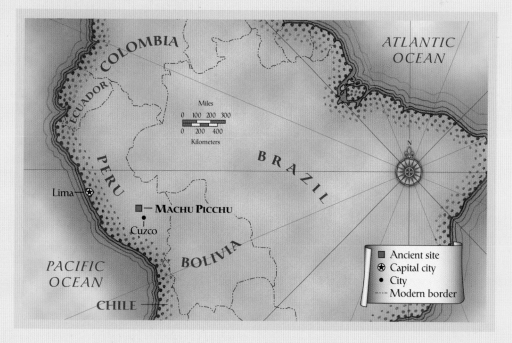

To feed mountain villages, the ancient Inca carved terraces into the mountainside for farming (above right). At Machu Picchu, stones and hand-carved blocks were placed one by one to form the walls and stairs (right) of this city in the clouds.

The land was about 7,875 feet (2,400 m) above sea level. It was so high that clouds often rolled in like blankets of fog. To reach this area, people had to climb steep, rocky slopes that were wet, slippery, and infested with poisonous snakes. They had to cross the roaring Urubamba River. Around them, mountain peaks in the Andes soared 18,000 feet (5,486 m).

Pachacuti did not build a palace in this rugged area—he built an entire royal village. This city in the clouds became known as Machu Picchu, named after the old mountain. It was built in about 1460 and had about 140 palaces, temples, houses, and other stone buildings.

KNOT *Writing*

The ancient Inca had no written language. So they used quipus to keep track of numbers. Quipus were lengths of colored, knotted string connected to one main string. Each color of string stood for a different item, such as the population of a village or the amount that village owed in taxes. A knot's position in the string stood for 1, 10, or other units. When a quipu was brought to the king, an expert would interpret the knots for him.

There were aqueducts to carry water for drinking, bathing, and cooking. Step-like terraces carved out of the steep mountainside gave farmers level land for growing crops.

WONDERFUL CONSTRUCTION

The ancient Incas left no written records. So we can only wonder how they built Machu Picchu. That task would have been difficult even with modern machines. The royal city was built with stone blocks as heavy as a car. The blocks are cut to fit together perfectly without the mortar needed in modern brick walls. Some blocks fit so snugly that a knife blade can't be forced between the joints.

Inca workers constructed buildings with carefully cut, perfectly placed stone blocks.

Water trickles through one of sixteen fountains that brought water to the residents of Machu Picchu. Inca engineers built a canal designed to bring freshwater from a nearby spring to feed the fountain system.

How workers lifted and moved the blocks is still a mystery. The Inca did not have wagons or other vehicles with wheels. But they somehow lifted hundreds of blocks high into the air to form walls and buildings. Scientists think they might have used ramps or rope cables.

Machu Picchu's water supply system also amazes modern engineers. It still works after more than six hundred years. People in the city needed water for drinking, cooking, and bathing.

One part of the system carried water from a spring to houses. Water flowed to houses in order of the importance of the occupants. First, it flowed into a stone tub where the king, or Sapa Inca, lived at the top of Machu Picchu. The stream of water from that tub flowed down through stone channels into the next house. Imagine living in the last house and getting dirty water that so many other people had used!

WONDERFUL CULTURE

The Inca civilization began as a small kingdom about two hundred years before Pachacuti took the throne. Within one hundred years after Pachacuti's death, however, the empire ruled ten million people. It stretched from the modern country of Colombia in the north for 2,500 miles (4,023 km) south into Chile.

> *"In one of [the] houses . . . they had more than twenty golden [llamas] with their lambs, and the shepherds with their slings and crooks to watch them, all made of the same metal. There was a great quantity of jars of gold and silver, set with emeralds; vases, pots, and all sorts of utensils, all of fine gold."*
> —Pedro de Cieza de León, a Spanish explorer, upon first entering the Inca capital of Cuzco in 1532

Inca rulers had fantastic amounts of gold and silver, but they probably did not use it as money. Instead, it went into statues, jewelry, and other works of art. That wealth was the Inca's downfall. Francisco Pizarro, a Spanish explorer, heard about Inca gold after arriving in 1532. He and his Spanish troops conquered the Inca to seize that gold.

The Inca culture disappeared as its people adopted the Spanish language, religion, and way of life. But the Spanish never reached Machu Picchu. It became a symbol of the Inca Empire.

This illustration by Belgian-born artist Theodore de Bry shows Incas bringing gold to the Spaniards to buy the freedom of their king in the 1500s. Although de Bry never visited the Americas, he based his series of engravings on written accounts and drawings by other European artists.

Local people continued to visit Machu Picchu. But people elsewhere forgot about Machu Picchu until a U.S. explorer named Hiram Bingham reached the area in 1911. Bingham called Machu Picchu the Lost City of the Incas. His magazine stories and books made millions of people aware of Machu Picchu and the ancient Inca civilization.

A MODERN WONDER

Machu Picchu has become the most famous symbol of the ancient Inca Empire. It is one of Peru's most popular tourist attractions. Almost five hundred thousand people visit it each year. Some people want to build hotels, a bridge or a cable car track leading to the mountain, and other facilities to allow more tourists to visit. Archaeologists worry that heavier tourism could damage Machu Picchu.

In 1911 American explorer Hiram Bingham, led by a Native American guide, came across Machu Picchu. Bingham is shown here camping at the site.

"I felt utterly alone. . . . Then I rounded a knoll and almost staggered at the sight I faced. Tier upon tier of Inca terraces rose like a giant flight of stairs. . . . Suddenly breathless with excitement, I forgot my fatigue and . . . I plunged once more into the damp undergrowth."

— *Hiram Bingham, on rediscovering Machu Picchu in 1911*

About ten million people living in Peru, Bolivia, and Ecuador still speak Quechua, the Inca language. While ancient ruins such as Machu Picchu are a fascinating symbol of a lost civilization, the survival of the Quechua language is one way in which this powerful culture lives on.

Visitors to Machu Picchu touch the Intihuatana, one of the Inca astrological tools. The stone, known as the hitching post of the sun, accurately predicts spring and fall equinoxes. On these days of equal day and night, the stone casts no shadow at midday.

EVER *Wonder?*

How did the ancient Inca honor their dead kings?

The ancient Inca turned the bodies of their dead kings—including Pachacuti—into mummies. They used special practices to preserve the hair, skin, eyes, and muscles after death. But they did not bury these royal mummies. They kept them in palaces and carried the mummies through the streets of Cuzco in parades. Living kings sometimes talked to the mummies, asking advice from past rulers.

$\mathcal{F}$RIAR JUAN DE SANTA GERTRUDIS WAS A SPANISH MISSIONARY IN SOUTH AMERICA IN 1758. AT THAT TIME, SPAIN RULED THE PRESENT-DAY COUNTRIES OF COLOMBIA, PANAMA, ECUADOR, AND VENEZUELA. MISSIONARIES SUCH AS FRIAR JUAN TRAVELED AROUND THOSE SPANISH LANDS. THEY TRIED TO GET NATIVE PEOPLE TO ADOPT THE CHRISTIAN RELIGION.

While traveling through southern Colombia, Friar Juan reached the tiny village of San Agustín. A few native families lived there. He expected it to be a simple farming village.

However, this village scared Friar Juan. Hidden among the trees were giant statues carved from stone. Some had huge heads with terrifying faces. Many looked part human and part jaguar. Their grins showed long, sharp fangs.

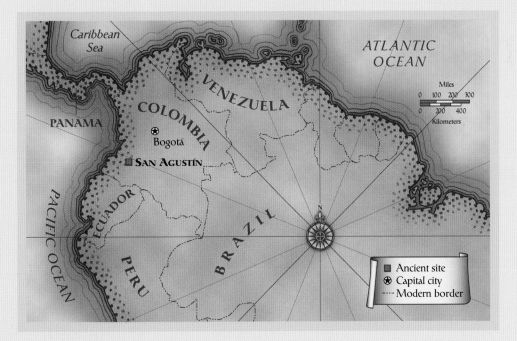

Left: *This detail from a painting by an unknown artist shows a ship carrying Catholic missionaries to the coast of South America in the 1700s.* Right: *A stone sculpture found at San Agustín. Little is known about the sculptures or the people who made them between the first and eighth centuries* A.D.

Some statues were almost 20 feet (6.1 m) tall. They could have looked right into the second-floor windows of a modern house. A number of the sculptures seemed to be standing guard near large mounds of earth. Many of the statues held clubs or axes and wore strange headdresses. Smaller statues showed monkeys, bats, birds, frogs, snakes, and other animals. Some were only 8 inches (20 centimeters) high.

The statues at San Agustín were carved from special kinds of rock. It was not hard rock like the granite found on some ancient monuments. The San Agustín carvers used light, soft rock called andesite and tuff. Some of this stone is soft enough to scratch with a fingernail. The carvers made chisels from harder rock and used those stone tools to make their statues.

DEVIL OF A DISCOVERY

Friar Juan had found one of South America's ancient wonders. He was the first person from Europe to write about the San Agustín statues. More than 500 statues and tombs have been found in the area. About 130 of the most important are located in what has become the San Agustín Archaeological Park.

This part of Colombia has the largest group of megalithic (large stone) statues in South America. These statues are spread out over a huge area. The park alone covers about 193 square miles (500 sq. km). More statues can be seen for miles around.

Friar Juan was convinced that the devil had carved those statues. He thought some of them looked like Spanish missionaries. But he could tell the statues had been in the area longer than Spanish people had. In addition, the people of San Agustín did not have iron tools with which to carve the statues. So it seemed reasonable that the devil was the sculptor. Maybe the devil wanted to warn the native people of the coming missionaries, Friar Juan thought.

The notes that Friar Juan had kept were not found until long after he died. For almost two hundred years, his description of the San Agustín wonders lay undiscovered. Several more European explorers visited this wild area after him. But most people in Europe and the United States weren't aware of San Agustín until the early 1900s.

"I am convinced that the Devil made these statues."
—*Friar Juan de Santa Gertrudis, the first European to write about the statues at San Agustín in 1758*

In 1913 German archaeologist Konrad Theodor Preuss arrived at San Agustín. Preuss and his team began the first scientific studies of the statues. The work he published later gave people in Europe and the United States their first glimpse of San Agustín.

Preuss counted and mapped the statues. He also studied the mounds of earth that some of the statues seemed to be guarding. Archaeologists discovered that those mounds were tombs where people had been buried. Some of the bodies were buried with gold and silver jewelry. The fierce-looking statues might have been built to scare away tomb robbers.

From these and later studies, we know that people from an ancient civilization built the San Agustín statues and tombs. People probably arrived in the area from other parts of Central and South America as early as 2,600 years ago. They gradually built a number of settlements into a great civilization.

Much of the ancient San Agustinian civilization remains a mystery. No written records were left to describe their history or how they lived. So archaeologists turned to artifacts (objects made by people) for information about the civilization. They studied stone carvings, tombs, and other objects that the San Agustinians left behind.

CITY FOR THE DEAD

Archaeologists think that the ancient San Agustinian civilization reached a peak between the first and eighth centuries A.D.

STEALING History

For centuries, looters (thieves) have stolen small statues and other objects from San Agustín. They also cut off the heads of some large statues. They sold those ancient objects to collectors. Looters also destroyed some tombs as they dug to search for buried gold and silver jewelry. Much of the stealing in recent years has happened outside the San Agustín Archaeological Park, where no guards protect the artifacts. Because of all the looting, the San Agustín statues are listed on the International Council of Museums' Red List of Latin-American Cultural Objects at Risk. This list names objects of historical value that are threatened by theft or damage from people. It helps museums, collectors, and others to identify and protect these items.

A stone statue guards the entrance to a tomb. Archaeologists believe that the ancient San Agustinian population had carved the fierce-looking statues to protect the tombs of their dead. But modern-day grave robbers haven't been scared off by such techniques.

Most of the sculptures were carved and the tombs built during this time. The civilization had vanished hundreds of years before Spanish explorers arrived in the area in the early 1500s.

The Chibcha people lived near this area when the Spanish arrived. Ancestors of the Chibcha might have founded the ancient San Agustinian civilization. San Agustín might have been built as their city for the dead.

San Agustinian people took great care to honor their dead. Some people were buried in simple graves under the floor of their huts. Rulers, priests, generals, and other wealthy people were buried in tombs. These special chambers were dug into the ground.

Some bodies were buried in a stone coffin, or sarcophagus. The sarcophagus was covered with a heavy stone slab before being placed into the tomb. Coffin lids sometimes were decorated with a carving of a person. It might have been an image of the person buried inside. Gold jewelry, small stone statues, and other objects often were buried with someone.

A broken stone sarcophagus was carved with the image of a human being.

This stone statue, carved with rounded eyes and jaguarlike teeth, still has remnants of paint used to call out its features.

FIERCE GODS AND GODDESSES

Once a body was inside a tomb, workers covered the grave with a mound of soil. Stone statues were placed outside the tombs. They might have been monuments to mark the location of a tomb. At the same time, the statues showed the power and wealth of the person buried inside.

Archaeologists think that some of the carvings represent gods and goddesses important in San Agustinian religious beliefs. Those statues might have protected the buried person from evil spirits. They also would have spooked grave robbers. Other statues might represent priests who had magical powers.

The bigger statues would have looked quite imposing in ancient San Agustín. Tall buildings did not exist there. Structures as large as the statues were unusual. The statues would have stood out even more because they were painted in bright colors. The paint faded over the years, leaving mostly bare stone for modern people to see. But archaeologists have found faint traces of red, yellow, black, and white paint on some of the sculptures.

"San Agustín represents a unique testimony to a vanished civilization."

—UNESCO, in naming the San Agustín Archaeological Park a World Heritage Site in 1995

A MODERN WONDER

Thousands of visitors see this modern wonder every year at the San Agustín Archaeological Park. People can explore the park on their own or go on guided tours. Tour guides explain the ancient history of the statues. Tourists also can see artifacts from the park at museums in Bogotá, the capital of Colombia.

Visitors to the park must obey rules that protect and preserve the statues. The rules forbid people from taking pieces of the statues away as souvenirs. However, statues also are located in many areas outside the park that are not protected.

In 1995 UNESCO named the park a World Heritage Site. This recognizes the park's importance for all of humanity. UNESCO's action encouraged the government of Colombia to protect and preserve the site so that this ancient wonder will exist for centuries to come.

A group of tourists poses with one of the statues found at San Agustín.

4 Tiwanaku

A father and son herd sheep along
a road overlooking Lake Titicaca
in Bolivia, where the ancient city
of Tiwanaku once existed.

$\mathcal{V}$ILLAGES NEAR LAKE TITICACA IN MODERN BOLIVIA AND PERU ARE AMONG THE POOREST IN SOUTH AMERICA. DAY AFTER DAY, PEOPLE STRUGGLE TO GROW ENOUGH POTATOES AND OTHER FOOD TO STAY ALIVE. PLANTS GROW POORLY IN THE SOIL. THIS RUGGED AREA IS 12,000 FEET (3,658 M) UP IN THE ANDES MOUNTAINS. AT THAT HEIGHT, OVERNIGHT FROST CAN FREEZE AND KILL PLANTS EVEN IN SUMMER.

But the ancient city of Tiwanaku flourished in this harsh climate. Tiwanaku was a prosperous city on the southern shore of Lake Titicaca, near the border of Bolivia and Peru. It was the capital of an empire that lasted for almost five hundred years, from about A.D. 500 to 1000.

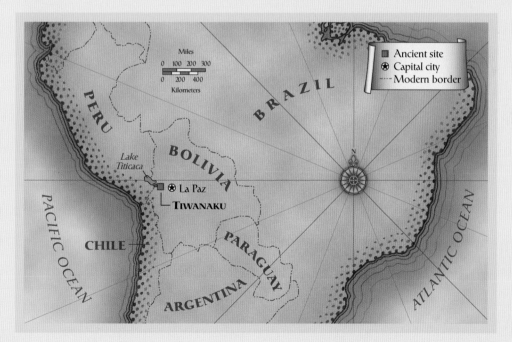

Tiwanaku is one of the most mysterious civilizations in the ancient world. With no written records, we don't even know what this civilization called itself. The name Tiwanaku (also spelled Tiahuanaco or Tiahuanacu) came from a more recent group that lived there. Experts think the name means "stone in the center." They think it was a way of calling Tiwanaku the center of the world.

EVER *Wonder?*

How do we know that Tiwanaku was a great empire?

Pottery and other artifacts made in Tiwanaku's unique style have been found great distances away, in modern Bolivia, Peru, and northern Argentina. Perhaps Tiwanaku covered this whole area, or maybe the empire was smaller and traded with civilizations far away.

More than fifteen hundred years ago, the civilization of Tiwanaku flourished on the shores of Lake Titicaca. During the 1800s and early 1900s, stone was removed from this site for building projects elsewhere. In the 1960s, attempts were made to restore the site, but early accounts by European visitors suggest that the original wall was made of freestanding statues spaced evenly apart.

Across from the walls of Tiwanaku's large temple is a sunken courtyard that served as another temple. Small stone faces are interspersed with the stone blocks of the walls of the courtyard.

PEOPLE WITH SQUARE HEADS

Archaeologists do know that the Tiwanaku people were great builders. The city was built from stone blocks, with no mortar needed to fill in gaps. The blocks were cut expertly to fit together on each side.

The stone came from quarries 25 miles (40 km) away. Archaeologists do not know how those blocks were cut, moved from the quarries to the city, or lifted into place to form buildings. Some of the stone blocks were so heavy that modern cranes would strain to lift them. They weighed as much as 110 tons (100 metric tons). That's about as heavy as fifty cars.

The Tiwanaku people also carved enormous humanlike stone statues. Archaeologists call them stelae, a word for carved stone pillars or slabs. One of these giants is 23 feet (7 m) tall. Each stela has a square head,

"The native told me . . . that all these marvels sprang from the ground in a single night. . . . There are not stones in any of the hills beyond."
—*Pedro de Cieza de León, the Spanish explorer, who visited the area in 1540*

square eyes, a rectangular mouth, and what looks like a helmet on its head. The tallest stela is in a museum in La Paz, Bolivia's capital city.

Other statues remain among the ruins of the ancient city. Walls of temples and a palace have also survived. The Ponce stela, at 8 feet (2.4 m) tall, still stands inside one temple. Not far off is a huge stone doorway known as Portada del Sol (Gateway of the Sun). A carving of the Tiwanaku god Viracocha stares down from the top of the gateway.

Nearby are remains of the largest Tiwanaku temple, the Akapana. Rising 50 feet (15 m) tall, this temple was like an earthen pyramid. Stone walls supported each of its seven levels. Sacrifices and other religious ceremonies were held on the top level. A system of tunnels let rainwater flow in and out of different levels of the pyramid. Archaeologists think the Tiwanaku built these tunnels to mimic mountain streams.

RAISING FIELDS

Growing conditions in the Andes are harsh. Early archaeologists wondered how the Tiwanaku people managed to feed a whole city. They did it by developing a new way of growing food, known as raised-field agriculture.

Top: *One of the larger-than-life-size stelae, known as the Fraile stela.* Above: *Portada del Sol was originally carved from a single block of stone 10 feet (3 m) high and 13 feet (4 m) wide. It weighs about 10 tons (9 metric tons).*

Tiwanaku farmers grew crops on raised beds that were irrigated by water-filled ditches (above). A vessel (left) from Tiwanaku depicting corn and yams dates to about A.D. 650.

This method enabled farmers to produce potatoes, fertilizer for the potatoes, and fish on the same land. Tiwanaku farmers must have been very intelligent to invent raised-field technology. It solved the big agricultural problems of this area: poor soil, cold weather, and lack of protein-rich foods.

In raised-field agriculture, Tiwanaku farmers piled up soil into rows called *suka kollus.* The rows were up to 3 feet (0.9 m) high, 10 feet (3 m) wide and 300 feet (91 m) long. The ditches between the rows were filled with water. The water irrigated the crops, and it also absorbed heat from the sun during the day. That kept the fields warm at night, reducing the risk of frost.

Farmers caught fish from ponds and streams and put them into the ditches. Then at dinnertime, they could catch fish to cook. The fish served another purpose too. They pooped in the water, producing a layer of rich fertilizer on the bottom of the ditch. Farmers scooped out that rich material. They used it to fertilize the soil in the raised rows. Plants and algae in the water also produced fertilizing material.

Some researchers have suggested that the ruined Puma Punku structure was a port with docks for boats that would have sailed on Lake Titicaca. Since the time of the Tiwanaku, the lakeshore has receded several miles.

Growing an Empire

Geographers discovered remains of these raised fields in the 1960s. They noticed the fields in photos taken from airplanes. The fields covered a huge area around Lake Titicaca. In the 1980s, archaeologists tested how effective Tiwanaku agriculture was. They rebuilt raised fields near Lake Titicaca and planted them with crops. In some areas, raised-field agriculture could produce about 22 tons (20 metric tons) of potatoes per hectare. The best modern agriculture, with fertilizers and pesticides, produced only about 15 tons (14 metric tons) in the same areas.

Raised-field agriculture provides naturally nutrient-rich soil for crops to grow. That could be partly why it works better. It also protects crops in areas prone to flooding. But studies show that the biggest advantage of raised fields is that they keep plants from dying during the area's frequent frosts.

Raised-field agriculture might have allowed Tiwanaku to grow from a small farming village around A.D. 200 into a powerful capital of the region. Before archaeologists discovered remains of the raised fields, they thought that only forty thousand people could have lived in Tiwanaku. But taking raised fields into account, they believe that there was enough food for five hundred thousand people.

Archaeologists do not know what happened to the Tiwanaku civilization. Some think that a long drought hit around 950. With less water, the Tiwanaku couldn't grow enough crops for their people. They moved to other areas to survive. The area had mostly been abandoned by the 1400s, when the army of the Inca Empire reached Tiwanaku.

The Inca might have copied Tiwanaku ways of building, farming, and running a government. Even though Tiwanaku was

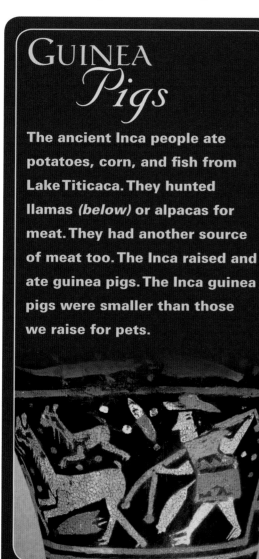

Guinea *Pigs*

The ancient Inca people ate potatoes, corn, and fish from Lake Titicaca. They hunted llamas *(below)* or alpacas for meat. They had another source of meat too. The Inca raised and ate guinea pigs. The Inca guinea pigs were smaller than those we raise for pets.

"I saw . . . many fine statues of men and women. So real they were that they seemed to be alive. . . . Women . . . [held] babies in their laps or bore them on their backs. In a thousand natural postures, people stood or reclined."

—Diego de Alcobaso, who visited ruins of Tiwanaku in the 1500s

empty when the Inca arrived, it was a very important conquest. Religious stories said that Tiwanaku was the place where the god Viracocha created the first people of the Andes Mountains. By controlling Tiwanaku, the Inca controlled the place where all their people had originated.

A MODERN WONDER

Only a few buildings still remain in Tiwanaku. People from nearby villages took some of the buildings apart and used the stone blocks for new buildings. Earthquakes destroyed other buildings.

Nonetheless, Tiwanaku is the most popular tourist attraction in modern Bolivia. Every year thousands of visitors from all over the world come to see the remains of this pre-Inca civilization. And in 1991, UNESCO named Tiwanaku a World Heritage Site as one of South America's greatest wonders.

The Aymara people living in the area around Tiwanaku still conduct religious ceremonies at the sacred site. Pictured is an Aymara priest conducting a ritual on June 21, the day of the winter solstice (shortest day of the year) in the Southern Hemisphere.

5 Tikal

$\mathcal{T}$HE ANCIENT CITY OF TIKAL LIES MOSTLY HIDDEN IN THE JUNGLE OF GUATEMALA. ONLY THE TALLEST BUILDINGS RISE ABOVE THE DENSE FOREST. BUT THIS HIDDEN CITY WAS ONCE THE LARGEST IN THE MAYA EMPIRE. THE EMPIRE STRETCHED FROM SOUTHERN MEXICO THROUGH HONDURAS.

During the peak of the ancient Maya civilization, from A.D. 200 to 900, Tikal probably was a nicer place to live than great European cities such as London and Paris. Residents of Tikal walked on paved streets, strolled broad paved plazas, and shopped for fresh fruits and vegetables in markets. Their rulers lived in magnificent palaces.

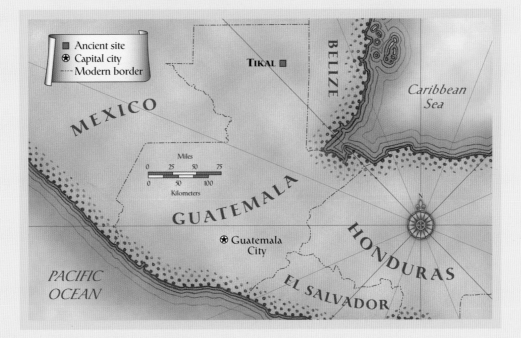

The Maya constructed the city of Tikal over several centuries. The bustling city was home to Maya royalty and served as a religious and cultural center.

Like other ancient Maya people, Tikal's residents built shrines and pyramid-shaped temples to worship their gods. They also made water reservoirs to irrigate their crops. The Maya created beautiful paintings and sculptures, and they were masters of mathematics and astronomy. They developed a system of writing with picturelike hieroglyphics. They even played a type of ball game. But games often had a serious purpose—and a bloody ending for the losing team.

PLACE OF SPIRIT VOICES

The name *Tikal* means "place of spirit voices" in the Maya language. Hieroglyphs carved in Tikal, however, call the city Mutal or Yax Mutal.

This photograph, taken in 1958, shows the Maya ruins surrounded by jungle. The ancient ruins were rediscovered by U.S. explorer John Lloyd Stephens in the 1800s. Major unearthing of the site took place between 1956 and 1970.

People lived in Tikal for almost 1,700 years, from 800 B.C. to around A.D. 900. With at least sixty thousand people by 700, Tikal became the largest Maya city. It covered about 25 square miles (65 sq. km) of land. About thirty thousand more people might have lived in villages around Tikal.

Around 900 something very mysterious happened to Tikal and other cities in the Maya Empire. People abandoned these cities. They moved away or died. Trees and vines from the nearby rain forest grew into and over the cities. Soon most evidence of the glorious Maya civilization had disappeared into the jungle.

Archaeologists are still trying to solve the mysteries of the ancient Maya. How did this civilization get started? How did the Maya live? Why did their great empire fall from power?

"Sometimes in my lonely chamber during the night I found myself so surrounded by roaring panthers with whom other creatures . . . mingled their cries, that I was forced to maintain a great fire at the entrance of my chamber, even occasionally to barricade it with timber."
—Teobert Maler, an early explorer of Tikal, describing his trip there in 1895

Tikal ruler Yik'in Chan K'awiil, also known as Ruler B, had the towering Temple IV built in 741.

MAGNIFICENT MAYA ARCHITECTURE

The temples built at Tikal were some of the most magnificent in the Maya Empire. These structures were pyramids built from limestone blocks. At the top were one or more small rooms used for worship and religious ceremonies. Some temple-pyramids were as tall as skyscrapers. Temple IV in Tikal is 212 feet (65 m) high, the height of a modern twenty-one-story building. It was the tallest building in the ancient Western Hemisphere.

Maya builders did not have iron or other metal tools to cut blocks for these buildings. However, they made tools from chert, a hard rock that could easily cut the softer limestone blocks. The Maya used another rock, obsidian, to make sharp knives, axes, arrowpoints, and other weapons.

ANCIENT KNIVES FOR *Modern Eye Surgery*

When modern eye doctors needed very sharp scalpels for eye surgery, they turned to the same material that the ancient Maya used for knives. That material was a glasslike rock called obsidian. Obsidian can be made into blades that are sharper than any other material. It was one of the most valuable materials in the ancient Maya Empire. New lasers have replaced scalpels for most modern eye surgery, but doctors sometimes still use obsidian scalpels.

Once the limestone blocks were cut, how did Maya workers move them? The ancient Maya never used the wheel, except in some toys. Without modern machines, how did workers raise the blocks up into the air to stack into walls? As with other ancient civilizations, this remains a mystery.

ROYAL PALACES

Maya rulers and their families lived in palaces. Some of the one-story structures had dozens of rooms and an open courtyard in the center, where residents and guests could sit in the sun and fresh air.

People also went to markets and religious ceremonies in Tikal's Great Plaza. The plaza was one of the largest paved areas in the world at that time.

Two enormous temples, Temple I and Temple II, stand at either end of the Great Plaza. This photo shows Temple I. In the center are the steps to the acropolis, which contains many stone buildings that may have housed Maya rulers and their families.

Top: *The Maya carved hieroglyphics—picture writing—into many of the buildings and stelae.*
Bottom: *A stucco mask of a Maya god decorates a pyramid at Tikal.*

It was about the size of a baseball diamond. Two temple-pyramids, tombs for Maya rulers, and stelae were built around the plaza. These stelae were carved on the front and sides with hieroglyphics. The hieroglyphics described the rulers of Tikal and the city's history.

Temple-pyramids, palaces, and other structures were covered with smooth plaster in ancient times. Many were painted in bright red and other colors. Most of that paint has worn off over the centuries, leaving just bare, worn stone. On some structures, plaster was sculpted into masks that are still visible.

"Some of the finest art ever done in the New World"
—*archaeologist Edwin M. Shook, describing Tikal in 1957*

EVER Wonder?

How do we know that blood was important in ancient Maya religious ceremonies?

Scenes carved on stone monuments and painted on pottery show kings and priests shedding their own blood during these ceremonies. They used sharp stingray spines and stone knives to pierce their tongues *(below)*, lips, ears, or other parts of the body. People believed that blood was the life source of their world. Spilling blood helped to keep the Maya world running and was a way to please their gods.

The Maya used temple-pyramids for bloody religious ceremonies. Enemy prisoners were captured during wars with other cities. Then they were taken to the top of a temple-pyramid. Maya priests cut open a prisoner's chest. They took out the heart as an offering to their gods, whom they believed controlled their crops. Sometimes the priests cut off the victim's head or spilled blood in other ways instead. They then let the body of the sacrificed person tumble down the pyramid steps.

A DEADLY GAME

Human sacrifices also were part of some ancient Maya ballgames. The Maya played on ball courts that usually were shaped like a capital *I*. Some courts were enclosed by slanting stone walls.

Players used a heavy ball made from the sap of rubber trees. The balls were about the size of a soccer ball, but they were not filled with air. They were solid rubber and weighed about 8 pounds (3.6 kilograms). That's as much as a gallon of water. Imagine doing a header with that ball!

Players had to wear padded clothing to protect themselves as they hit the ball back and forth to one another. Nobody is certain about the rules.

Maya ballplayers wore elaborate costumes, headdresses, and lots of padding.

In some games, players tried to keep the ball in the air by hitting it with their hips. Sometimes they bounced the ball off the slanted walls of the ball court or tried to bounce the ball through a hoop on the wall.

The game might have been played just for fun at times. However, it also was played as a part of religious holidays, to celebrate victories in war, and on other important occasions. On these occasions, the losing team or their leader might be killed.

A MODERN WONDER

Tikal is part of modern Guatemala's Tikal National Park. It was the first national park in Central America. Many of Tikal's temple-pyramids and other buildings have been restored, and thousands of tourists flock to Tikal each year to visit such places as the Temple of the Great Jaguar. It is the tomb of Tikal's greatest king, Jasaw Chan K'awiil I (often called Ruler A).

More than three thousand buildings and 250 stone monuments still remain among the forest in Tikal. Satellite photos have shown that there may be up to four thousand Maya sites deep in the jungles that archaeologists have not yet uncovered.

The Temple of the Great Jaguar, also known as Temple I, was built in 730. It contains the body of Jasaw Chan K'awiil I, who lived from 682 to 734. He had Temple II built for his wife, nicknamed Lady Twelve Macaw.

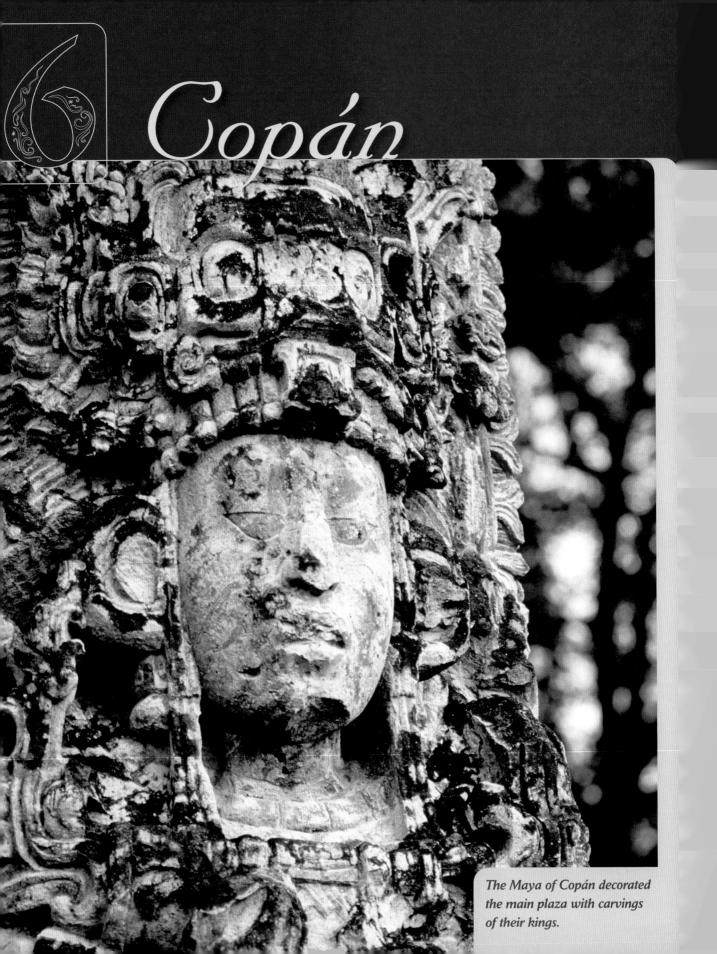

6 Copán

The Maya of Copán decorated the main plaza with carvings of their kings.

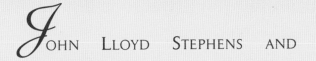

$\mathcal{J}$OHN LLOYD STEPHENS AND FREDERICK CATHERWOOD WERE STRUGGLING THROUGH THE RAIN FOREST IN HONDURAS IN 1839. THESE EXPLORERS HAD HEARD ABOUT RUINS OF AN ANCIENT MAYA CITY HIDDEN IN THE JUNGLE. THEY SET OUT IN SEARCH OF THE MYSTERIOUS PLACE. THEIR GUIDES USED SHARP MACHETES (LARGE KNIVES) TO CUT A PATH THROUGH DENSE JUNGLE VINES AND BUSHES.

The forest was immensely thick and shady. "We could not see 10 yards [9 m] before us, and never knew what we should stumble upon next," Stephens said. Bushes had sharp thorns and leaves that could blister the skin worse than poison ivy. Screeching green parrots, toucans, and other birds flew through the air. Troops of howler monkeys leaped from tree to tree overhead.

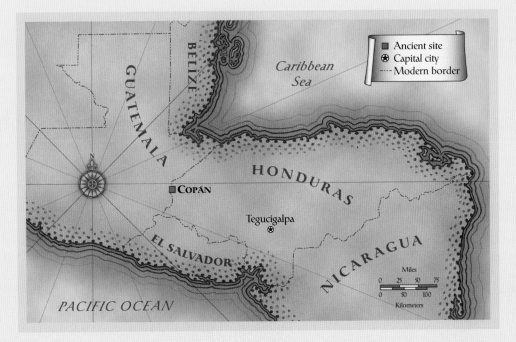

Frederick Catherwood created a series of drawings of several ancient Maya cities he encountered with John Lloyd Stephens in the mid-1800s. This illustration shows Copán as they found it in 1839.

When Stephens and Catherwood reached the ancient city, known as Copán, the ruins reminded them of a shipwreck. "It lay before us like a shattered bark [boat] in the midst of the ocean, her masts gone, her name effaced [erased], her crew perished, and none to tell whence she came, to whom she belonged, how long her voyage, or what caused her destruction," Stephens later wrote.

As Stephens explored Copán, he noticed carvings in the stone monuments. Stairs leading up one temple in particular were covered in hieroglyphics and ancient portraits. "One thing I believe," he wrote. "[The history of Copán] is graven [carved] on its monuments. Who shall read them?"

"We sat down on the very edge of the wall, and [tried] in vain to penetrate the mystery by which we were surrounded. Who were the people that built this city? . . . America, say historians, was peopled by savages. But savages never reared these structures, savages never carved these stones."

—*John Lloyd Stephens, who rediscovered Copán in 1839*

The Hieroglyphic Stairway (above) *is covered with hieroglyphics* (detail below) *telling of the life and times of many ancient Maya rulers.*

HISTORY BOOK OF STONE

Stephens was correct about the Hieroglyphic Stairway. Archaeologists later realized that the stairs were a history book written in stone. Around twenty-two thousand hieroglyphs cover more than sixty stone steps. The staircase is one of the world's longest texts carved in stone, and it is the longest ancient Maya text ever discovered. It tells the history of the kings of Copán, beginning with the ruler named Great Sun First Quetzal Macaw, who founded the city in around 426.

Over the years, Copán grew in size and power, reaching a population of about twenty thousand. Its rulers ordered construction of huge plazas, temple-pyramids, palaces, sculptures, paved streets, and more. Archaeologists believe that Copán's buildings were as beautiful as those in the greatest cities in ancient China, India, and Egypt. Some even called it the Athens of the Maya World, after the great Greek city.

By the 500s, Copán had become the government center for other cities and villages in the surrounding countryside.

Hieroglyphics carved into Copán's staircase and on other Maya structures have helped experts understand this civilization. Experts used to think that the Maya were a peaceful people. But hieroglyphs and murals have shown that warfare among cities was very common.

The Maya also used their hieroglyphic writing in hundreds of books called codices. These books were made from the inner bark of fig trees and folded up like fans. They contained information about one thousand years of Maya history. However, settlers from Spain who conquered the Maya in the 1500s did not understand the codices. Spanish settlers thought the books were evil and burned hundreds of them. Only four ancient Maya codices survived. They explain the ancient Maya

DINNER *Dogs?*

The ancient Maya kept dogs, parrots, and a raccoonlike animal called the coatimundi as pets. However, they raised some dogs for meat, just like we raise chickens and turkeys. Dog meat is rich in protein, which was lacking in other Maya foods. Eating cooked dog meat helped the ancient Maya survive.

This is a section from the Madrid Codex, one of the four surviving codices from Maya history. The information contained in the codices has helped scientists understand the ancient Maya culture, religious beliefs, and ways of life.

> *"We found a large number of books in these characters and, as they contained nothing in which there was not to be seen superstition and lies of the devil, we burned them all, which they [the Maya] regretted to an amazing degree, and which caused them affliction."*
>
> —*Diego de Landa, a Spanish priest who thought ancient Maya codices were witchcraft and burned many of these books in 1562*

calendar and Maya beliefs about astronomy. Experts first deciphered the Maya number system by studying these books.

Ever Wonder?

Why did archaeologists dig deeper and deeper after discovering ancient Maya ruins?

Because excavating (digging out) Maya temples or homes is like turning pages of a history book. When the owner of a house died, relatives tore it down and built a new house on top of the wreckage. They sometimes buried the owner in the wreckage. By excavating each layer, archaeologists can find skeletons and artifacts from further and further back in Maya history.

KING 18-RABBIT

Archaeologists began identifying ancient Maya rulers before they could fully translate Maya hieroglyphics. They learned that one king of Copán started construction of a temple, known as Temple 26, in the early 700s. They called the king 18-Rabbit, using English words for the pictures in his name hieroglyph. They have since learned his real name was Waxaklajuun Ub'aah K'awiil. But the name 18-Rabbit is still used because it is easier to say.

In 738 another city defeated Copán in a war. King 18-Rabbit was killed before the stairway was finished. A later king ordered completion of the Stairway in 755. When finished, it told the story of the entire ruling family of Copán.

Earthquakes are common in this region. Over time, earthquakes shook Copán and knocked down many of the stairs. Only about thirty remained in their original place. With the other hieroglyphics jumbled and out of order, archaeologists had an extremely difficult time understanding the story written in stone.

However, translation of the hieroglyphics gave us important information about the ancient Maya. The text told how the Maya Empire was divided into two parts in the 600s. One area was ruled by Tikal in Guatemala and the other by the city of Calakmul, which was located in Mexico about 60 miles (97 km) north of Tikal.

Scientists continue to hunt for clues to the ancient Maya civilization.

Something happened at Copán after 800. People abandoned the city, leaving a ghost town. The same thing occurred throughout the Maya Empire around this time. We do not know why. People might have been killed in wars, which were happening more and more often. Droughts might have caused food shortages. Perhaps several such events occurred at once, bringing an end to the powerful ancient Maya Empire.

A MODERN WONDER

More than six million Maya descendants live in modern Central America, Mexico, the United States, and elsewhere. Many of them still speak Maya languages similar to those spoken at Copán and other sites.

Parts of Copán have been restored as part of Copán National Park. The park attracts thousands of visitors each year. Archaeologists are still working to uncover and restore tombs and other structures around Copán that may help solve the mysteries of the ancient Maya.

7 BRAZILIAN Stonehenge

ODERN ASTRONOMERS STUDY PLANETS AND STARS FROM OBSERVATORIES. THESE DOME-SHAPED BUILDINGS HAVE POWERFUL TELESCOPES AND OTHER INSTRUMENTS FOR OBSERVING OBJECTS BILLIONS OF MILES AWAY. BUT OBSERVATORIES ARE NOT A NEW CONCEPT. SCIENTISTS HAVE LEARNED THAT PEOPLE IN ANCIENT CIVILIZATIONS BUILT TYPES OF ASTRONOMICAL OBSERVATORIES THOUSANDS OF YEARS AGO.

In 2006 archaeologists in Brazil discovered the ruins of one of the oldest observatories in the Western Hemisphere. They believe it was built between five hundred and two thousand years ago.

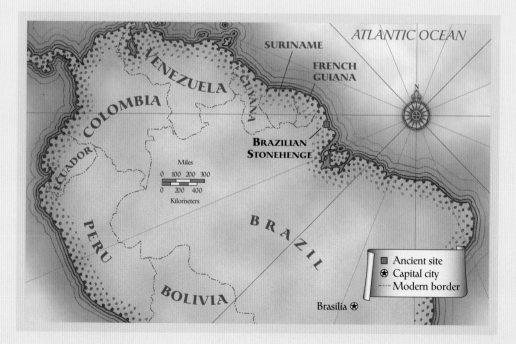

Above: *Scientists explored the site of the Brazilian ruins in May 2006. The ruins suggest that a fairly advanced ancient civilization once lived there.* Below: *The stones that make up the observatory are massive blocks of granite. Some are taller than people.*

Located on a hill in the northern state of Amapá, this ancient structure did not look anything like modern observatories. It consisted of 127 stone blocks placed upright in the ground. The blocks, up to 9 feet (2.7 m) tall, were arranged in a circle about 100 feet (30 m) in diameter. Residents of the nearby village of Calcoene had known about the blocks for years. But scientists recently became interested when they flew over the area in a helicopter and noticed that the stones formed a circle.

Archaeologists realized that the structure wasn't a natural formation—people had built it. Then they discovered that on the same day each year, December 21, the shadow of one of the blocks disappears when the sun is directly overhead. They believe this must have been an observatory to keep track of the sun and stars.

TIME TO CELEBRATE

Why would ancient people have wanted to mark this date? December 21 is the winter solstice, when the sun is lowest in the sky. It is the start of winter and the shortest day of the year in the Northern Hemisphere. (Although much of Brazil is in the Southern Hemisphere, where the seasons are reversed, these ruins lie in the Northern Hemisphere.) Ancient people in Brazil and elsewhere in Central and South America might have needed to mark the solstice for a variety of reasons.

The solstice would have been very important for agriculture. Experts think the ancient people of this area kept track of the sun, the moon, and the stars to know when to plant and harvest crops. In the tropical Amazon rain forest, they had to plan for a long rainy season. Intense rain falls there from late December until August.

This civilization might also have held important religious ceremonies on the solstice. Celebrations around the solstice happen all over the world.

Many familiar holidays, including Christmas and Hanukkah, are celebrated around the time of the winter solstice.

Researchers began calling the site of the observatory the Brazilian Stonehenge. The original Stonehenge is an ancient circle of stones in England. Some scientists think that ancestors of the Palikur Indians built the Brazilian Stonehenge. Until recently, nobody thought that those ancient people had the knowledge to build such a structure.

The observatory suggests that ancient people in the Amazon might have been more advanced. They must have been able to record the sun's movement for years and build with stone blocks that each weighed more than a car.

THE FIRST *Stonehenge*

Stonehenge is an ancient stone monument in southern England. It was built between 3000 B.C. and 1800 B.C. from thirty upright stone pillars. Each pillar weighed about 26 tons (24 metric tons). Flat slabs of stone rest on top of the pillars to form a ring. Inside is a smaller ring of stones made in the same way. On June 21, the summer solstice, the sun rises behind one stone and seems to balance on top of the stone.

The ancient site in Brazil got its name because it reminded scientists of another ancient site— Stonehenge in England (left).

Observatories in the Ancient American World

This observatory certainly is not the only ancient observatory in Central and South America. Cities such as Copán and Tikal in the ancient Maya Empire had dozens of observatories. Rulers designed homes and temple-pyramids with more than one purpose in mind. These buildings were places to live or worship gods but also to observe the movements of the sun, the moon, and the planets. The Maya used that information to develop a calendar. The Maya calendar was one of the most complex and accurate ever invented.

In recent years, archaeologists have discovered another observatory, known as Chankillo, in Peru. This structure was built in the 300s B.C., making it the

A satellite view of Chankillo, located in Peru. The concentric circles on the upper left may have served as either a fortress or a stone temple. From there, thirteen stone towers can be seen on the ridge to the right. When the sun rises on the winter solstice (in June in Chankillo), the sun aligns with Tower 1.

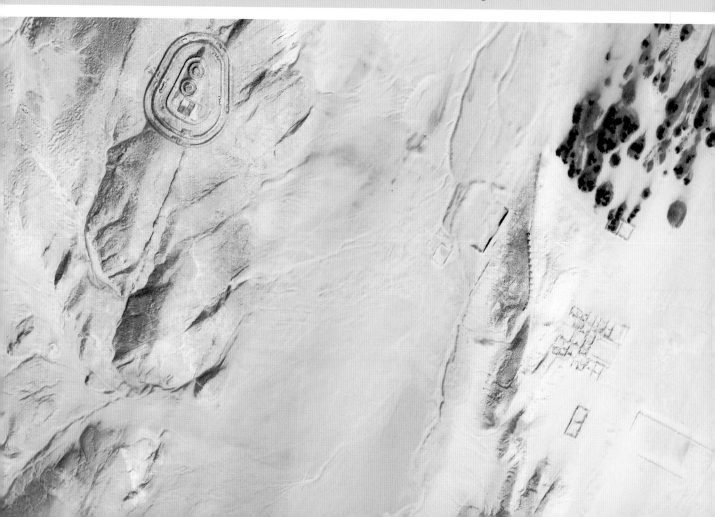

"Only a society with a complex culture could have built such a monument."
—archaeologist Mariana Petry Cabral, of the Amapá Institute of
Scientific and Technological Research

oldest known observatory in North America or South America. It includes thirteen towers that line up with the rising and setting of the sun at various points of the year. The people of the Andes noted the places where the sun rose and set to keep track of the year.

Ancient observatories had no domes, telescopes, or other scientific instruments. In some cases, doors or windows were the instruments. Builders might have carefully positioned a window, for instance, so that the sun would rise through it on a certain day of the year. One small window in the west wall of Temple 22 in Copán was positioned so that it faces the setting sun on April 12. That was the start of spring planting for Maya farmers. The sun in the window told farmers that planting time had arrived.

We know from these observatories that ancient civilizations not only collected scientific information but used it in their daily lives. Astronomical observations helped the Maya survive by planting crops just in time to get the best yields during the rainy and dry seasons. Astronomy also

Left: *A carved Maya calendar. The Maya calculated one solar year (the time it takes for Earth to travel around the sun) to be 365 days. Their year consisted of eighteen months of twenty days each plus five extra days.*

determined when they held ceremonies, crowned new kings, and made other important decisions.

A MODERN WONDER

Scientists may not fully understand the Brazilian Stonehenge for years. They need more information about how the ancient Amazonian people used it. Many other questions about this discovery still lack definite answers. Who built the Brazilian Stonehenge? When exactly was it built? How did these ancient people cut and move such huge rocks?

In modern times, fewer than one thousand descendants of the ancient Palikur people live in Brazil. The Brazilian Stonehenge is in a remote area that is difficult to reach. However, tourists can visit the structure and marvel at this ancient wonder. As scientists keep learning about the ancient cultures of the Americas, they hope to unravel more of the mysteries of the Brazilian Stonehenge.

TIMELINE

CA. **2000 B.C.**	Early Maya culture begins to develop.
800 B.C.	The Maya settle in the area that later became Tikal.
200 B.C.	The Nazca civilization develops along the south coast of Peru.
A.D. **0–100**	The people of San Agustín, Colombia, started carving megalithic statues.
200	The village of Tiwanaku on Lake Titicaca starts to grow and develop. The Maya civilization begins to thrive in cities such as Tikal.
426	The Maya king Great Sun First Quetzal Macaw founds the city of Copán.
500	The civilization at Tiwanaku flourishes.
600	The Nazca civilization collapses.
700s	The San Agustín civilization declines and stops carving stone statues.
755	Several years after Copán's King 18-Rabbit was defeated, a later king orders the completion of the Hieroglyphic Stairway.
800s	The Copán civilization declines, and the city is abandoned.
900	Tikal is abandoned.
1000–1100	The Tiwanaku Empire collapses.
1200	The Inca settle in the Cuzco Valley of modern-day Peru.
1438	Pachacuti takes the throne as the Inca king.
CA. **1460**	Machu Picchu is built near Cuzco, Peru.
1492	Christopher Columbus sails to islands in the Caribbean Sea. News of his "discovery" of the New World generates more interest among other Spanish explorers.
1520s	Hernán Cortés invades Mesoamerica, enslaving the Maya and exploiting all their resources.
1532	Francisco Pizarro and his troops defeat the Inca Empire but never find Machu Picchu in Peru.
1758	The Spanish missionary Juan de Santa Gertrudis discovers ruins of San Agustín.
1839	Explorers John Lloyd Stephens and Frederick Catherwood discover the ruins of Copán.
1848	The Maya ruins of Tikal are accidentally discovered.
1895	Teobert Maler, an explorer and photographer, is one of the first to study and document the Tikal ruins.
1911	Hiram Bingham discovers Machu Picchu.

1913 German archaeologist Konrad Theodor Preuss begins the first archaeological study of the statues at San Agustín.

1926 Toribio Mejía Xesspe sees the Nazca lines from a hilltop in Peru.

1946 Maria Reiche begins to investigate the Nazca lines, convinced they are connected to Nazca study of astronomy.

1960s Geographers flying over land near Lake Titicaca notice patterns in the ground—the remains of ancient raised-field agriculture.

1980s Scientists work with farmers living near Lake Titicaca to rebuild raised fields. Crop yields are much higher than in traditional farming.

1984 Scientists show that geoglyphs like the Nazca lines could be drawn fairly quickly and easily without a pattern.

2006 Archaeologists discover the Brazilian Stonehenge.

CHOOSE AN EIGHTH WONDER

Now that you've read about the seven wonders of ancient Central and South America, do a little research to choose an eighth wonder. Or make a list with your friends, and vote to see which wonder is the favorite.

To do your research, look at some of the websites and books listed in the Further Reading and Websites sections of this book. Look for places in Central and South America that
• *have a cool history*
• *were difficult to make at the time or required new technology*
• *were extra big or tall*
• *were hidden from view or unknown to foreigners for many centuries*

You might even try gathering photos and writing your own chapter on the eighth wonder!

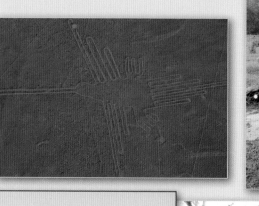

8

GLOSSARY AND PRONUNCIATION GUIDE

archaeologist: a scientist who studies buildings, tools, and other remains of ancient civilizations

artifacts: objects, especially tools, weapons, or art, remaining from earlier civilizations

Brazilian Stonehenge: remains of what archaeologists believe is an astronomical observatory built by an ancient culture in Brazil

Central America: the narrow strip of land that connects Mexico and South America

Copán (koh-PAHN): one of the main cities of the ancient Maya Empire, located on the border between Honduras and Guatemala

culture: the values, beliefs, customs, and way of life of a group

empire: lands brought together under a single government or ruler

geoglyphs: lines and pictures drawn in the ground

hieroglyphics: a system of writing that uses pictures and symbols

Machu Picchu (MAH-choo PEEK-choo): an ancient royal city in the mountains of Peru, built by the powerful and advanced Inca civilization

megalithic: made with huge stones used in ancient cultures as monuments or building blocks

Mesoamerica: a geographical area that spans from Mexico into Central America

Nazca (NAS-kuh) lines: large-scale lines, shapes, and figures etched in the ground in the desert of Peru in ancient times. They are so big that their shapes are recognizable only from high above.

San Agustín: an archaeological park (and nearby town) in Colombia that is the site of hundreds of stone statues carved by an ancient civilization

stela (STEE-luh, plural stelae STEE-lee): a carved stone slab or pillar made to honor and remember a person or event

Tikal: one of the main cities of the ancient Maya Empire, located in Guatemala

Tiwanaku (tee-wah-NAH-koo): a town in Bolivia, near Lake Titicaca; home to an ancient civilization that invented raised-field agriculture

United Nations Educational, Scientific and Cultural Organization (UNESCO): a branch of the United Nations, an international organization devoted to cooperation between countries. UNESCO's World Heritage Centre identifies and helps protect and preserve sites that are part of the world's cultural and natural heritage

Source Notes

11 Jim Woodman, *Nazca: Journey to the Sun* (New York: Pocket Books, 1977), 23.

13 Maria Reiche, *Nazca Lines: Mystery on the Desert* (Lima: Peruvian Airministry, 1949), 23.

21 Piedro de Cieza de León, quoted in PBS, "Ice Mummies of the Inca: Lost Empire," *NOVA Online*, November 2000, http://www.pbs.org/wgbh/nova/peru/worlds/empire2 .html (January 16, 2008).

22 Hiram Bingham, quoted in Richard E. Bohlander, ed., *World Explorers and Discoverers* (New York: Da Capo Press, 1998), 54.

27 Friar Juan de Santa Gertrudis, quoted in Gerardo Reichel-Dolmatoff, *San Agustín: A Culture of Colombia* (London: Thames and Hudson, 1972), 24.

32 UNESCO. "World Heritage List: San Agustín No. 744," October 10, 1994, 14. http:// whc.unesco.org/archive/advisory_body_evaluation/744.pdf (February 12, 2008).

37 Pedro de Cieza de León, *The Second Part of the Chronicle of Peru* (London: Hakluyt Society, 1883), 36–50.

40 U.S. Library of Congress, "Bolivia: Historical Setting," 2005, http://lcweb2.loc.gov/ cgi-bin/query/r?frd/cstdy:@field(DOCID+bo0012) (February 20, 2008).

42 Diego de Alcobaso, quoted in Harold T. Wilkins, *Mysteries of Ancient South America* (New York: Citadel Press, 1956), 188.

47 Teobert Maler, "Jaguar in the Night," *Mesoweb*, 2006, http://www.mesoweb.com/ maler/jaguar.html (April 8, 2007).

50 Edwin M. Shook, quoted in Willam G. Weart, "Expedition Finds Data on Mayans; 2,000-Year-Old Secrets of Lost Civilization Discovered in Tikal, Guatemala," *New York Times*, May 26, 1957, 9.

55 John Lloyd Stephens, quoted in Rebecca Stefoff, *Finding the Lost Cities* (New York: Oxford University Press, 1997), 55.

56 Ibid., 54.

56 John Lloyd Stephens, quoted in PBS, "Transcripts: Lost King of the Maya," *NOVA Online*, February 13, 2001, http://www.pbs.org/wgbh/nova/transcripts/2804maya.html (March 22, 2007).

56 John Lloyd Stephens, quoted in Michael D. Coe, *America's First Civilization* (Washington, DC: American Heritage Publishing, 1968), 138.

59 Diego de Landa, quoted in Robert Sharer, *The Ancient Maya* (Palo Alto, CA: Stanford University Press, 1994), 513.

65 Michael Heckenberger, quoted in Stan Lehman, Associated Press, "Archaeologists Discover Brazilian 'Stonehenge,'" June 28, 2006, http://www.livescience.com/ history/060628_ap_brazil_stonehenge.html (February 22, 2007).

68 Mariana Petry Cabral, quoted in Rhett Butler, "Amazon Stonehenge Suggests Advanced Ancient Rainforest Culture," *Mongabay.com*, May 14, 2006, http://news.mongabay .com/2006/0514-amazon.html (February 22, 2007).

SELECTED BIBLIOGRAPHY

Bahn, Paul G., ed. *Cambridge Illustrated History: Archaeology*. Cambridge: Cambridge University Press, 1996.

Bohlander, Richard E., ed. *World Explorers and Discoverers*. New York: Da Capo Press, 1998.

Burton, Rosemary, and Richard Cavendish. *Wonders of the World: 100 Great Man-Made Treasures of Civilization*. New York: Metro Books, 2003.

Cantor, Norman F. *Antiquity: The Civilization of the Ancient World*. New York: HarperCollins, 2003.

Coe, Michael D. *America's First Civilization*. Washington, DC: American Heritage Publishing, 1968.

Diamond, Jared. *Collapse: How Societies Choose to Fail or Succeed*. New York: Viking, 2005.

Fash, William Leonard. *Scribes, Warriors and Kings: The City of Copán and the Ancient Maya*. London: Thames and Hudson, 2001.

Katz, Friedrich. *The Ancient American Civilizations*. Edison, NJ: Castle Books, 2004.

Reader's Digest Editors. *Vanished Civilizations*. New York: Reader's Digest, 2002.

Renfrew, Lord, and Paul G. Bahn, eds. *The Cambridge Illustrated History of Archaeology*. Cambridge: Cambridge University Press, 1999.

Scarre, Chris, ed. *The Seventy Wonders of the Ancient World: The Great Monuments and How They Were Built*. London: Thames and Hudson, 2000.

Stefoff, Rebecca. *Finding the Lost Cities*. New York: Oxford University Press, 1997.

Westwood, Jennifer. *Atlas of Mysterious Places*. London: Marshall Editions, 1987.

FURTHER READING AND WEBSITES

Books and Magazines

A Day with a Maya. Minneapolis: Runestone Press, 2000. Learn about the life of the native peoples of Mesoamerica through facts and fiction.

Ash, Russell. *Great Wonders of the World*. New York: Dorling Kindersley, 2000. This title looks at both ancient and modern constructions. The maps, diagrams, and illustrations give readers a glimpse into the beautiful buildings of the world.

Calvert, Patricia. *The Ancient Inca*. New York: Franklin Watts, 2004. This book explains the civilization and culture of the Inca people. The builders of the magnificent city of Machu Picchu, the Inca excelled in building roads and bridges through formidable mountain passes.

Day, Nancy. *Your Travel Guide to Ancient Mayan Civilization*. Minneapolis: Twenty-First Century Books, 2001. This book discusses the lifestyle and customs of the ancient Maya. You'll learn how they dressed, what they ate, which gods they worshipped, and more.

Gruber, Beth. *Ancient Inca: Archaeology Unlocks the Secrets of the Inca Past*. Washington, DC: National Geographic, 2006. See vivid National Geographic photos of the infamous "Ice Maiden" and marvel at the beautiful pottery and textiles created by the Inca.

Kops, Deborah. *Machu Picchu*. Minneapolis: Twenty-First Century Books, 2009. This title in the Unearthing Ancient Worlds series details the re-discovery and excavation of Machu Picchu by explorer Hiram Bingham and his crew.

——. *Palenque*. Minneapolis: Twenty-First Century Books, 2008. John Lloyd Stephens and Frederick Catherwood found several Maya cities, including Copán and Palenque, on their travels through Central America. Kops tells of their journey as well as the excavations and discoveries at Palenque by archaeologist Alberto Ruz Lhuillier and his team.

Lewin, Ted. *Lost City: The Discovery of Machu Picchu*. New York: Philomel Books, 2003. Lewin uses watercolors to illustrate the wonders of Bingham's journey into the jungles and mountains of Peru in 1911.

McIntosh, Jane. *Eyewitness Books: Archaeology*. New York: Alfred A. Knopf, 1994. The author provides a broad overview of the field of archaeology with easy-to-understand explanations of how scientists learn about other civilizations. Photographs of many artifacts and sites provide an exciting picture of earlier civilizations.

Moloney, N. *The Young Oxford Book of Archaeology*. New York: Oxford University Press, 1997. This title explains how archaeologists excavate a site and the methods used to document their findings.

O'Neill, Catherine. "Lost Worlds." Chapter in *Amazing Mysteries of the World*. Washington, DC: National Geographic Society, 1983. The author explains the significance of Machu Picchu and the Nazca lines in Peru, as well as many temples in Mexico.

Woods, Michael, and Mary B. Woods. *Ancient Construction: From Tents to Towers.* Minneapolis: Twenty-First Century Books, 2000. Read how the Mesoamerican civilizations achieved great archaeological feats—including Maya saunas—without the use of the wheel.

———. *Seven Wonders of Ancient North America.* Minneapolis: Twenty-First Century Books, 2009. Explore such wonders as the Mesa Verde Cliff Palace in Colorado and the ancient Aztec city of Tenochtitlán, Mexico, in this book detailing ancient sites in North America.

Websites

Annenberg Media Exhibits: Collapse
http://www.learner.org/exhibits/collapse/index.html
This site helps students understand how actions and inactions affect history. Click on "The Maya" to discover possible causes for the collapse of Copán.

The Maya Ruins Page
http://www.mayaruins.com
View photos from a number of ancient sites in Mesoamerica, including Tikal and Copán. Choose a site to visit by clicking on a place-name on the map.

Mystery of the Maya
http://www.civilization.ca/civil/maya/mminteng.html
The Canadian Museum of Civilization created this site, where you can see some of the ancient Maya exhibits that the museum presented in the 1990s.

Odyssey Online: Ancient Americas
http://carlos.emory.edu/ODYSSEY/AA/aaflashfront.htm
This is a fun, interactive site sponsored by the Michael C. Carlos Museum of Emory University and Memorial Art Gallery of the University of Rochester. Explore the trivia on this site to learn what makes this civilization so fascinating!

Smithsonian.com: Winter Palace
http://www.smithsonianmag.com/travel/winter.html
This travelogue provides an account of Hiram Bingham's discovery of Machu Picchu and also describes the enormity of the wonders of the ancient city.

A Woodworker's Bench Notes: Pattern Making
http://www.benchnotes.com/Pattern%20Making/Pattern_Making.html
Find out how to use grids to enlarge patterns, which is one possible way the Nazca people drew their intricate lines.

World Heritage List
http://whc.unesco.org/en/list
UNESCO maintains this site, listing the natural and cultural sites of the world that should be protected. See which sites have been named World Heritage Sites, and find out why they are culturally and historically significant.

INDEX

About the Authors

Michael Woods is a science and medical journalist in Washington, D.C., who has won many national writing awards. Mary B. Woods is a school librarian. Their previous books include the eight-volume Ancient Technology series, the Disasters Up Close series, *The History of Communication*, *The History of Medicine*, and *The Tomb of King Tutankhamen*. The Woodses have four children. When not writing, reading, or enjoying their grandchildren, the Woodses travel to gather material for future books.

Photo Acknowledgments

The images in this book are used with the permission of: © age fotostock/SuperStock, pp. 5, 18 (bottom), 19, 38 (both); © Tom Till/Photographer's Choice/Getty Images, p. 6; © Laura Westlund/Independent Picture Service, pp. 7, 17, 25, 35, 45, 55, 63; © Kevin Schafer/Alamy, p. 8; © British Museum/Art Resource, NY, p. 9 (top); © Werner Forman/Art Resource, NY, p. 9 (bottom); © Keystone Pictures Agency/ZUMA Press, p. 10; © iStockphoto.com/Jarno Gonzalez Zarraonandia, pp. 12, 72 (top center); AP Photo/Alejandro Balaguer, p. 13; © Kevin Schafer/CORBIS, p. 15; © Mark Harris/Stone/Getty Images, pp. 16, 72 (bottom left); © David Madison/The Image Bank/Getty Images, p. 18 (top); © JTB Photo Communications, Inc./Alamy, p. 20; © Bildarchiv Preussischer Kulturbesitz/Art Resource, NY, p. 21; © Roger-Viollet/The Image Works, p. 22; © Roswita Misselhorn/Gallo Images/Alamy, p. 23; © Jane Sweeney/Art Directors, pp. 24, 33; The Art Archive/Museo Nacional Bogota/Gianni Dagli Orti, p. 26 (left); © Pep Roig/Alamy, p. 26 (right); © Mauritius/SuperStock, p. 29; © Michael Freeman/CORBIS, p. 30; © Jack Barker/Alamy, p. 31; Ben Wiedel-Kaufmann/Janine Wiedel Photolibrary/Alamy, p. 34; © PCL/Alamy, p. 36; © Mary Jelliffe/Art Directors, p. 37; © Kenneth Garrett/Danita Delimont/Alamy, p. 39 (top); © Pre-Columbian/The Bridgeman Art Library/Getty Images, p. 39 (bottom); © Martin Gray/National Geographic/Getty Images, p. 40; The Art Archive/Cusco University Museum/Mireille Vautier, p. 41; © Aizar Raldes/AFP/Getty Images, p. 43; © Wilbur E. Garrett/National Geographic/Getty Images, p. 44; © Warren Jacobs/Art Directors, p. 46; © Fritz Goro/Time & Life Pictures/Getty Images, p. 47; © Karl Buhl/Danita Delimont/Alamy, p. 48; © iStockphoto.com/Brian Raisbeck, p. 49; © Upperhall/Robert Harding World Imagery/Getty Images, p. 50 (top); © John R. Kreul/Independent Picture Service, p. 50 (bottom); The Granger Collection, New York, p. 51; © Justin Kerr, K1209, p. 52; © Peter McBride/Aurora/Getty Images, p. 53; © Kevin Schafer/Stone/Getty Images, p. 54; © Newberry Library/SuperStock, p. 56; © Charles & Josette Lenars/CORBIS, p. 57 (top); © Craig Lovell/CORBIS, p. 57 (bottom); © The Print Collector/Alamy, p. 58; © Kenneth Garrett/National Geographic/Getty Images, p. 60; AP Photo/Governo De Amapa, Gilmar Nascimento, p. 62; © Gilmar Nascimento/AFP/Getty Images, pp. 64 (both), 72 (top right); © Skyscan Photolibrary/Alamy, p. 66; © GeoEye/SIME, Courtesy of NASA, p. 67; © iStockphoto.com/Hannah Gleghorn, p. 68; © Craig Lovell/Eagle Visions Photography/Alamy, p. 72 (top left); © Cindy Miller Hopkins/Danita Delimont/Alamy, p. 72 (center right); © Jane Sweeney/Lonely Planet Images/Getty Images, p. 72 (bottom center); © Sybil Sassoon/Robert Harding World Imagery/Getty Images, p. 72 (bottom right).

Front Cover: © Gilmar Nascimento/AFP/Getty Images (top left); © iStockphoto.com/Jarno Gonzalez Zarraonandia (top center); © Mark Harris/Stone/Getty Images (top right); © Jane Sweeney/Lonely Planet Images/Getty Images (center); © Sybil Sassoon/Robert Harding World Imagery/Getty Images (bottom left); © Craig Lovell/Eagle Visions Photography/Alamy (bottom center); © Cindy Miller Hopkins/Danita Delimont/Alamy (bottom right).